LAFLIN'S LAUGH-LINES

By Duane Laflin

A collection of fun and funny stuff for entertainers, emcees, teachers, preachers, and public speakers

A product of LAFLIN MAGIC
Box 3003
Troy, Montana 59935
406-295-7790

Published by:

Winters Publishing
P.O. Box 501
Greensburg, Indiana 47240
800-457-3230

© 2002 Duane Laflin

All rights reserved
Printed in the United States Of America

Material in this book may be used in performance by those who purchase it. Apart from that, no part of the book is to be photocopied or reproduced by any other means. Please do not send portions of this book out over the internet.

Library Of Congress Control Number 2002107781
ISBN 1-883651-20-4

CONTENTS

Introduction 4
Sources 6
Section One: Warm-ups and Wake-ups 7
What Are Warm-ups and Wake-ups 8
Chapter One: A Warm-up - "Meet My Pa" (Paw) 10
Chapter Two: A Warm-up or Wake-up
 "If It Wasn't For You" 12
Chapter Three: A Warm-up or Wake-up
 "Clap Hands Stunt - Number One" 14
Chapter Four: A Warm-up or Wake-up
 "Clap Hands Stunt - Number Two" 16
Chapter Five: A Warm-up - "The Exact Distance" 18
Chapter Six: A Warm-up or Wake-up - "The Group Hug" .. 20
Chapter Seven: A Wake-up - "Moving An Audience" 22
Chapter Eight: A Warm-up or Wake-up - "Thumb-Body" 24
Chapter Nine: A Warm-up - "The Right Foot" 26
Chapter Ten: A Warm-up or Wake-up
 "Tickled To Life" 27
Chapter Eleven: A Warm-up or Wake-up
 "Group Impressions" 30
Chapter Twelve: A Wake-up - "Your Body Is A Machine" .. 32
Chapter Thirteen: A Warm-up - "The Wilting Flower" 34
Section Two: Comedy Lines 37
About The Comedy Lines 38
Various Comedy Lines .... 39 - 94

INTRODUCTION

In 1990, I published a book titled *Comedy Collection For Introducing Gospel Themes*. The book was well received. It is now out of print.

When first written, that book was intended for use by those who present specific messages. The jokes were "lead-in" material for a subject or topic that would be part of a speech or lesson.

In October of 1994, I did a revision of that original book and turned it into something that would serve a more general purpose. The "lead-in" aspect of the book was dropped, while more and different lists of themed jokes were added. A special feature of the book was the fact that the jokes were grouped under unique topics and key concepts.

The new book was called *Duane's Comedy Concepts*. It also was well received. It also is now out of print.

Now it is 2002, and I find myself referring to my own copies of those two books when preparing speeches, presentations, and performances. As well, I see that my personal collection of comedy lines and themed jokes has grown far beyond what is in those two books.

This led me to the conclusion that it is time for another book of comedy lines. It will contain revised and expanded material from the earlier books, plus a gathering of humorous ideas that I have not yet put in print.

This new book will also contain material from a third book. We released *Favorite Warm-ups* in 1993. It was a series of funny greetings and silly stunts that involve an entire audience. This book was very popular and sold out quickly.

Since *Favorite Warm-ups* is also out of print, and since it had a strong emphasis on humor and entertainment, I've decided to let it mesh with this latest publication of comedy material.

So, you now have in your hands the result of compiling, changing, and enhancing three earlier works, plus adding in new humor content and laugh lines. The intent has been to create a helpful resource that will be of value to anyone who is interested in bringing laughs and a good time to a crowd of people.

There are three purposes this book can help those who make vocal presentations to the public achieve:

1. The development of bits and extended jokes for use in emcee work. A Master Of Ceremonies often needs several lines, rather than one joke, to fill between acts. He or she is also occasionally in need of some entertaining bits of business that involve the audience at large. Such things are contained on these pages.
2. The development of patter that creates transitions. Performers who entertain from the stage or small platform often need things to say that assist in a segue from one presentation to another. Staging or prop requirements may create gaps of time that need to be filled with clever words or interesting comments.
   Almost every kind of speaker or entertainer needs a way to fill silent or empty spots that occur when scenes are being set, or when a program is faced with unexpected delays. The material in this book is well suited for turning what otherwise could be an awkward pause, into a brief and enjoyable interlude.
3. The development of new comedy material. Clowns, story tellers, magicians, ventriloquists, jugglers, and even preachers are usually on a continual search for new gags, bits, and lines that can be added to their act (or sermons).
   Much of what is on these pages can be turned into short segments that will enhance larger routines.

The format is simple. The first part of the book is devoted to "Warm-ups" and "Wake-ups." The rest of the book is categorized jokes. Read it for the fun of looking over the lines. Read it to discover comedy ideas that can be adapted to your own work.

Duane Laflin - April, 2002

Sources

It is good to give credit where credit is due. This is something that is easier said than done. Many times, no one knows the source of a joke or funny idea. Beyond that, sometimes several people claim to be the originator of the same idea and it is difficult to know who actually thought of it first.

Making things even more complicated, there are occasions when several different people, working independently, do come up with the same concept and therefore, all deserve some credit.

I will do my best to mention those who shared ideas with me that I am passing on. When aware of a source, I am pleased to declare it. However, you will find that I do not identify many sources. This is because most of the sources are doubtful or unknown.

I admit that I am not the creator of most of the funny stuff in this book. I have done the topical arranging. There is room for me to claim some originality about the matter of putting particular comedy lines together under good themes. None of the sequences in this book were copied or consciously "borrowed" from others.

I also may have refined some of the gags and lines. Definitely, a few of the jokes and audience participation stunts were "thought up on my own," and it really is a pleasure to have created a few things that audiences seem to appreciate.

But overall, this book is a collection of things that have been tossed around by many people for many years.

I am grateful for all those who keep jokes alive and repeat funny stuff. It makes it possible for smiles and laughs to happen more than once. I'm also pleased that such things are repeated with enough frequency that a person who is willing to try to write it all down can soon have a large file under the subject of humor.

The aim is to pass along a portion of the stuff that has accumulated in my pile and file of funny business. A large portion of the concepts in this book didn't begin with me and will not end with me. I'm passing them along!

SECTION ONE

WARM-UPS AND WAKE-UPS

What Are Warm-ups And Wake-ups?

A person performing for groups of people, or charged with the responsibility for giving leadership to a large crowd, may find himself in this difficult situation: the audience really isn't ready to watch and listen.

Maybe the preliminaries have gone on too long. Maybe an inexperienced emcee has wearied the people with rambling jokes and reminiscences. Possibly, there has been an overly long award ceremony which, when combined with a banquet, has resulted in full stomachs and slightly sleepy people.

Whatever the cause, the performer or leader finds himself needing to get the attention of the audience. At the same time, he also needs to provide some sort of change of pace that will refresh the group and prepare them to focus on the presentation that will follow.

This is where the "warm-up" becomes an extremely helpful tool. It is an action or short activity that involves the entire audience. It allows the crowd to physically move, and usually provides the opportunity for a smile or laugh. It is a technique that could be likened to "shifting the gears." It changes the sense of energy in a room.

Since a "warm-up" is not simply a matter of telling people to "stand up and stretch," it also establishes or reinforces the leadership of the person in charge.

When people stand up and stretch, they also tend to start talking to those who are next to them, rather than listening to what a leader has to say. They also will do such things as decide it is time for a trip to the bathroom. If they are tired, they may even think it is the opportunity to sneak to the door for an early exit from the program.

Using a "warm-up" will keep a leader in command. It accomplishes the same purpose as does having people stand up and stretch, but it also keeps their attention focused. It allows the leader to establish a good working relationship with his or her audience by providing an experience that both entertains and revives.

A "warm-up" also gives the audience a message about physical response. Because people are asked to follow certain actions which are clearly meant to be fun, they get the idea that laughter and applause are in order.

A "wake-up" is similar to a "warm-up." Actually, the two things can be used interchangeably. The only difference is timing. A "warm-up" is normally used near the start of a program, or even before it officially starts. A "wake-up" occurs sometime during the event.

If a room is hot and stuffy, people may get drowsy in spite of the leader or performer's best efforts to keep them alert. There are many factors that can cause an audience to become distracted or weary. Being able to pause in the midst of a presentation and do something fun, something that allows the audience to rise to their feet and move around, while still accepting direction from the presenter, is a wonderful thing.

That's what the "wake-up" does. It helps people with wandering minds or tired attitudes tune in again to what is happening. It accomplishes this by way of an interesting and pleasurable (sometimes goofy) event that actually seems to be part of the program.

When "wake-ups" and "warm-ups" are used properly, an audience doesn't even realize the true purpose of such activities. They will be simply viewed as clever entertainment tools, planned comedy experiences, or greeting exercises.

Finally, "wake-ups" and "warm-ups" are important tools when working with churches. When doing a program in front of a congregation, you may find that people aren't used to clapping or even laughing out loud. They may be unsure about an appropriate response for your program. (In some churches, people in the pews rarely make any kind of response to what happens on the platform. They view their role as that of only being quiet listeners and observers. If you want more than that out of them, you need to clue them in.)

A good audience participation gag can set an audience free to express appreciation and enthusiasm.

Now that you know what "wake-ups" and "warm-ups" are, it is time to get down to business. The following chapters are specific audience participation events for you to use in your programs.

Chapter One: A Warm-up
"MEET MY PA" (PAW)

This idea was shared with me by Hubert Ryan of Toronto, Canada at the Torbuff (Toronto - Buffalo) conference for the *Fellowship Of Christian Magicians* in May of 1993. He created the gag. It is printed here with his permission and blessing.

I have used the idea with much success.

The humor is of the "groaner" variety, and that is just fine. A magician by the name of Daryl has said, "A good groan can be an excellent form of audience participation."

HOW TO DO IT:

Ask the audience to stand. While they do so, explain that they must not say anything or do anything apart from standing up.

Once the people have risen to their feet, instruct them all to turn and face someone. As a joke you may comment, "Hopefully, facing someone won't be too unpleasant of an experience."

When everyone has found someone to look at, tell them to extend their right hand toward the other person. Tell them not to let their hands touch. They only are to reach toward the person.

Next, ask everyone to say to the other person, "HAVE YOU MET MY MOTHER?" Because it is such a strange thing to ask of a stranger, this usually gets a laugh.

After everyone has asked the question (they do it all at the same time), tell them to follow it up by saying, "NOW...MEET MY PA! This is a play on words which means shake hands...MEET PAWS.

Many people will get the joke immediately, and start shaking hands. The people who don't get the joke won't want anyone to know they don't get it, so they, too, will laugh and shake hands.

The result is friendly greetings and light-hearted comments about the silly, yet fun, nature of the joke.

As an effort to make sure all in the audience appreciate the pun, it doesn't hurt to elaborate. Once you allow time for people to catch the play on words and start shaking hands, you can go ahead and give an explanation for those who may yet be in the dark. Say, "Pa means paw, as in hand. You know, p-a-w. Meet paws. Shake hands. Introduce yourself. Go ahead, make a new friend!"

Finish with this announcement: "Now that you have all met paws, you may be seated!"

People do enjoy this humorous way of being set up for shaking hands and meeting someone next to them. When they sit down, they will do so with a sense of enthusiasm about the rest of the program.

Chapter Two: A Warm-up or Wake-up
"IF IT WASN'T FOR YOU!"

This exercise is a pleasant event that produces smiles and good feelings. As a means of getting people to say "hello" to one another, you may want to use it at the start of an event.

It also is effective as a bit of funny business that can take place at any time during a presentation.

HOW TO DO IT:

My preference is to ask the audience to stand while this takes place, but in many situations I have done it while people were yet in their seats, and it still worked fine.

If you do ask the audience to stand, tell them not to start any conversation. Whenever they are asked to stand as a group, people have a habit of beginning to talk. To keep from losing their attention, it is important to explain that another instruction will soon be given, and it is necessary to stay quiet so it can be heard.

Ask the audience to turn and find someone to look at. Often it is wise to suggest that they look toward someone they don't know. Tell them this could be the opportunity to make a new friend.

Once everyone has found someone to look at, tell them to repeat the following to the other person: "IF IT WASN'T FOR YOU" (pause while the group says this much), "I WOULD NOT BE STARING AT" (pause again so they can say this), "THE NICEST PERSON IN THIS ROOM" (give them time to say these words). "I WANT TO SHAKE YOUR HAND!"

Encourage them to go ahead and shake hands. Finally, you say, "Now that you all have met the nicest person in the room, you may be seated!"

SECOND VERSION:

This other way to use the gag is more fun, but some audiences may not appreciate it. Evaluate your audience and try to decide the humor quotient that is present before doing this.

Have the audience stand and do everything as with the first version, only with this exception, rather than having them say, "I would not be staring at the nicest person in this room," have them say, "I WOULD NOT BE STARING AT...THE MOST ATTRACTIVE PERSON IN THIS ROOM! I WANT TO SHAKE YOUR HAND!"

This usually gets a big laugh, especially if you have teenagers in the group.

Don't let the simplicity of this gag fool you. It really is a winner.

Chapter Three: A Warm-up or Wake-up
CLAP HANDS STUNT - NUMBER ONE

Clowns have been doing this one for years. I have no idea who first thought of it.

It works with the audience either seated or standing.

HOW TO DO IT:

Announce that everyone must do exactly as you do. Children will automatically play along with you. Teens and adults occasionally respond to it slowly. You may have to tease a bit and say something such as, "Come on now, I realize you are sophisticated, dignified, and mature, but this will be good for you. You might think of it as a brief aerobics exercise."

Then, extend your arms in front of you. Instruct the crowd to do this with their arms. Once the audience stands before you with arms extended, count "ONE" and swing your hands together with a loud CLAP. Clasp your hands when they meet. Then, deliberately "unclap" your hands by pulling them apart and continuing to hold them out in front of you.

Make sure the audience has tried to do this along with you. They should also have made a big CLAP and then separated their hands. Remind them that it is vital for them to do as you do.

Do it a second time. Forcefully CLAP your hands together as you count "TWO." This time the crowd should be right with you. They, too, will clap their hands.

Again, deliberately "unclap" your hands by pulling them back apart and continuing to hold them out in front of you. The audience will follow your example.

For a third time, swing your hands together as you shout "THREE!" But this time, purposely MISS THE CLAP so your hands just silently swing by one another.

The crowd will not be expecting this. In their effort to quickly follow your directions they will have anticipated a third CLAP, so they actually will CLAP their hands.

Next, the audience will laugh at their mistake and the fact that you surprised them.

With a smile and twinkle in your eye, tell them that it is important to pay careful attention to what is happening. They must do exactly as you do.

Offer to give everyone a second chance. Tell them the exercise will be repeated.

Do as you did before with the first CLAP. Then separate your hands.

This time, MISS THE CLAP on the second effort. Let your hands swing by one another when you shout "TWO," rather than waiting for "THREE."

Once again, the people will be caught by surprise. They will be expecting you to miss the clap on three, so when you say two, they will CLAP their hands when they aren't supposed to. There will be even more laughter.

Conclude the event with a comment like this, "Well, folks, you didn't do exactly as I did, but you made a good attempt. I give you all an "A" for the attempt, so why not give yourselves a round of applause?"

I have found that a nice way to introduce this gag is by saying it is "TIME FOR A GROUP EXPERIMENT." Comment that you are going to give the audience a simple test. Then, when it is over you can say, "Please give yourselves a round of applause for putting up with the experiment. Now, let's get on with the show!"

Readers who do magic shows may want to end the gag by saying, "Have you heard the expression that THE HAND IS QUICKER THAN THE EYE? Apparently, your hands are quicker than your eyes. You saw what I did, but your hands moved too fast to stop."

From that statement the performer may then go on to give another demonstration of sleight of hand, which would be one of his or her actual tricks.

Chapter Four: A Warm-up or Wake-up
CLAP HANDS STUNT - NUMBER TWO

This is another thing that I learned from watching clowns. It has been done in many ways and used in a variety of situations.

It is another exercise that can be done with the audience either seated or standing. My preference is to have them stand.

Instruction is given that everyone should put his or her HANDS OUT IN FRONT OF HIS OR HER BODY WITH THE PALMS FACING EACH OTHER.

The performer then explains that whenever the signal is given, the audience is to clap once. The CLAP is demonstrated by vigorously swinging the hands together to make a loud noise. The audience is given a chance to practice this making of a loud CLAP.

Next, the signal is demonstrated. The performer turns sideways and stretches his arms away from his body. His left hand is aimed low toward the floor, his right hand is aimed high toward the ceiling. With a quick movement, he changes the position of his hands. This means his right hand is now aimed toward the floor and his left hand is aimed at the ceiling.

The performer explains that WHENEVER HIS HANDS PASS BY ONE ANOTHER, that is the moment when the audience members are to clap their hands once. They must not clap when his hands start moving. They must only clap at the specific moment when his hands pass by one another.

The audience is given the opportunity to practice this. The performer changes the position of his hands so they pass by one another. He does this slowly. When the hands pass by each other, the people clap.

This matter of "clapping on signal" is practiced a few times.

Finally, the audience is told it is time to "keep up with the performer," and the funny business begins.

He passes his hands by one another more quickly. The people clap. He does it again (quickly) and the people clap. Then he moves his hands quickly as if he is going to cross his hands, but actually HE DOES NOT. He stops his hands short of actually passing by one another.

This will catch the audience off guard, and, since they were expecting the performer's hands to actually pass by one another as they had previously, they will clap.

The performer says, "Remember what I said. You must only clap at the signal. Don't clap when my hands move. Only clap when they pass by one another. If my hands cross, you clap. If they don't cross, you don't clap. Let's try it again!"

From this point on, the performer sometimes actually lets his hands pass by one another, then other times he tries to "fake out" the audience by acting like his hands will cross, but keeping them from really doing so.

People enjoy this. It is fun to try to keep up with the performer and funny to see themselves, and those around them, messing up most of the time.

After a series of hits and misses, the performer starts CROSSING HIS HANDS AT A VERY QUICK PACE. No misses now, just quick CLAPS. It starts to sound like an ovation!

Then, the signal is stopped and the audience is told, "What a pleasure to hear such wild, enthusiastic, and sincere applause. Thank you very much."

Along with this being simply a fun thing to do, it is practical for situations (such as churches) wherein people may be unsure about whether or not applause is allowed during the program. It educates them immediately that for this particular presentation hand clapping is completely in order.

Chapter Five: A Warm-up
THE EXACT DISTANCE

Without doubt, this stunt is a groaner. Nevertheless, the physical activity involved does give the audience a chance to move around. More than that, the joke is so corny people can't help but chuckle. When it ends, they are shaking hands and giving one another a compliment which means, in spite of the silliness, this gag achieves positive results.

HOW TO DO IT:

The audience must stand. Each person is then requested to face another person. From this position each person is to LOOK TOWARD THE OTHER PERSON'S SHOES.

While continuing to look down, each person is told to step back EXACTLY ONE INCH. No one will be sure how much an exact inch is, but everyone will move around a bit and most will grin about having to follow such an instruction.

After being asked to move back one inch, the audience is next told to STEP TO THE RIGHT, EXACTLY ONE INCH. Again, there will be some confusion about how to do this, but people will try and there will be smiles in the process.

When the movement stops, ask the audience to carefully notice the situation. Tell them to observe that EACH OF THEM IS NOW EXACTLY THE SAME DISTANCE APART. Tell them to notice that YOUR FEET ARE EXACTLY THE SAME DISTANCE FROM THE OTHER PERSON'S FEET...THAT THE OTHER PERSON'S FEET ARE FROM YOURS!

This is an absurd observation. Obviously, all will automatically be the same distance apart, no matter how far they have moved. However, it may take a moment for this to dawn on some.

As people begin to realize that this entire exercise is just a joke, tell them, "I know, it is a silly thing to notice, but let's put it to good use. Instead of looking at the person's feet, now look him or her in the eye and say...'YOU KNOW, WE MUST BE IN EXACTLY THE RIGHT PLACE'." (Give them time to say this.)

Also tell them to REACH ACROSS THE GAP BETWEEN THEM AND SHAKE HANDS. As they do so they are to say, "Thank you for being smart enough to be here. We obviously are in EXACTLY the right place."

This should result in people pleasantly introducing themselves to one another.

As you request them to be seated, you may remark, "Today we really are in exactly the right place, and we going to have a terrific time together."

Chapter Six: A Warm-up or Wake-up
THE GROUP HUG

Don't let the title of this gag bother you. No psychobabble here, just funny business.

This is something that came to me "on the spot." I was doing a program for children wherein they were supposed to understand a mirror image. In the process of trying to explain the concept, I hit upon the idea of having them copy my actions, only in reverse. The natural ending to the series of backwards copycat motions was a hug.

HOW TO DO IT:

Begin by telling the audience that they must act like a mirror. This means, whatever they see you do, they must do in reverse. This is what mirrors do. They reflect what they see from an opposite perspective.

RAISE YOUR RIGHT HAND. Say, "When I am looking in a mirror and raise my right hand, what hand do I see going up? RAISE THE PROPER HAND!" (Typically, many in the group don't understand yet, so will raise their right hands.)

"No, I would not see the right hand go up. I would see the hand directly across from my right hand rise. In this mirror this would be the left hand. Are you confused? To do what a mirror would do, you must do the reverse of what I do. So, if my right hand is up, your left hand should rise up. Then it would be a matching reflection."

This is not as complicated as it seems. Actually, the audience enjoys it. There are usually some giggles as people find themselves trying to figure out which hand to put up. Adults tend to like this even better than do children, mainly because they don't catch on to it as quickly as do the children, so end up laughing at themselves.

"Now that we know how to do it, let's try it again. RAISE YOUR LEFT HAND." A large portion of the audience will have been expecting you to raise your right hand again, so will again be briefly confused. Once they get the proper hand up, bring your left hand down and raise your right hand again.

NEXT RAISE BOTH HANDS. (Comment about this motion being easy.) THEN REACH ACROSS YOUR BODY WITH YOUR LEFT ARM. Keep your arm there. Your left hand grasps your right shoulder.

Give people time to figure this out. They have fun trying to move in the opposite direction that you do. They should end up with their right arm grasping their left shoulder.

WHILE KEEPING YOUR LEFT ARM IN PLACE, REACH UP WITH YOUR RIGHT ARM TO GRASP YOUR RIGHT SHOULDER. Give the audience time to copy this. NOW GIVE YOURSELF A SQUEEZE. Audience members give themselves a squeeze.

When you squeeze yourself, say, "AH!" Tell the audience to say it, too. Once everyone has done so, finish the event with these words, "Ladies and gentlemen, you have just experienced what we call a *group hug*. I hope you all feel better. You may be seated."

I can't leave this gag without urging you to give it a try. On paper it may not appear to be something that would entertain a group of people. After years of putting the idea into practice, I can say from experience that it is very entertaining. I don't understand why people like it so well. I never would have expected them to respond to it so well, but they do.

Chapter Seven: A Wake-up
MOVING AN AUDIENCE

Here is another groaner, but people will smile when it happens. It is a great way to relax and refresh a crowd through physical movement.

This is also another old idea. It is a commonly known gag that has been around for many years (although I have never seen it in print). I have no idea who thought of it first.

HOW TO DO IT:

Ask your audience to stand. Once the group is on its feet, tell everyone to lean to the right. Once they do this, ask them to lean to the left.

Next, ask them to lean forward. Then, ask them to lean backwards. When asking them to lean backwards, warn them not to go too far. Stress that they must not lose their balance.

Follow this by having them rise up on their toes and then return to a regular standing position. If you are so inclined, you might take them through the entire routine again.

People will follow your directions with curiosity. By the end of the actions they will be trying to figure why you are having them do these things. This means they are ready for the punch-line.

Address the crowd and say, "It is said that a sign of a good communicator is having the ability to *move* an audience. I think you can all say that you were just *moved*. In fact, why not turn to the person next to you and, along with giving him or her a handshake, say...'You know, I was just moved'."

Next you might say, "And now, please be so moved as to take your seats."

This stunt is very good to use when you sense that the audience is uncomfortable. As we said in an earlier chapter, there are many reasons why audiences at times have difficulty focusing on a presentation. When faced with such an occasion, this gives you a means of having them stand up and get some exercise that will help them be more alert.

At the same time, because of the punch-line, it appears to be a form of entertainment. For all they know, the joke was pre-planned.

Please don't overlook the comment about warning the people, when asking them to lean backwards, not to go too far. I learned this the hard way. When I first started using the gag, in nearly every show someone would fall over. You wouldn't think people would be so foolish as to follow a leader's directions to such an extreme, but they will do it.

So, when you ask the crowd to lean backwards, quickly and immediately say, "But not too far. Make sure you don't fall over."

Chapter Eight: A Warm-up or Wake-up
THUMB-BODY

This is my favorite of all the warm-up and wake-up gags. It can be used at any time during a program. The audience may be either seated or standing.

HOW TO DO IT:

Instruct everyone to hold their arms out in front of them and then STICK THEIR THUMBS UP. You set the example for this by doing the same. Put your arms out in front of you with your thumbs sticking up.

Once everyone is in this position, turn your hands so the THUMBS POINT SIDEWAYS and ask everyone to do the same. Then, POINT YOUR THUMBS DOWNWARDS and ask everyone to do the same. Next, go ahead and POINT YOUR THUMBS UPWARDS AGAIN and ask everyone to do the same.

How long you repeat the above sequence is up to you. It seems to work well if you go through it several times, each time a bit faster. The people do their best to keep up with you.

Finally, pause and ask this question, "DO YOU KNOW WHAT WE ARE ALL DOING?" Allow the audience a brief moment to ponder the matter, then tell them, "WE ARE DOING THUMB-THING!" (Something) This gets a laugh, but there is more...

While they are still laughing or groaning about the pun, tell them, "Wait, it's not over. Now turn to someone nearby and with YOUR THUMB TOUCH HIS OR HER THUMB." Give them time to do this. Now ask, "DO YOU KNOW WHAT YOU ARE DOING NOW?" Again, allow a brief moment for the question to be pondered. "YOU ARE MEETING THUMB-BODY!" (Somebody)

"Since you have just met thumb-body, you might as well shake hands and say to the person, 'You are thumb-body special'."

Conclude the event by saying, "Now that you have all met thumb-body special, you may be seated."

This "thumb-body" gag has never received anything but a positive response. Usually, it prompts much laughter.

In these days of political correctness, I've wondered if anyone would ever view the joke as making fun of a speech impediment. It certainly does not do that. It is only meant to be a play on words. A pun.

Anyway, since modern audiences seem to be often peppered with plenty of critics, I've thought someone someday might not approve of the stunt. I'm glad to report that it hasn't happened. I've never had anyone misunderstand the intent, or fail to enjoy the innocent fun.

Chapter Nine: A Warm-up
THE RIGHT FOOT

This one needs to be used as a warm-up. It wouldn't make sense to use it at any time other than early in a program. It is another idea that has been around for a long time. It is a short, sweet, and humorous event that many have used with success.

HOW TO DO IT:

Ask the audience to stand. Once everyone is on his or her feet, tell them to "LIFT YOUR LEFT FOOT UP OFF THE FLOOR." Once they do this, say, "Put it back down."

Do it a second time. Instruct the crowd to again "LIFT YOUR LEFT FOOT UP OFF THE FLOOR." After they follow the instruction, say, "Put it back down."

For a third time say, "LIFT YOUR LEFT FOOT UP OFF THE FLOOR." Once they do this, tell them, "NOW, PLEASE DO A QUICK HOP!"

Wait for this to happen; then deliver the punch-line, "LADIES AND GENTLEMEN, THEY SAY IT IS IMPORTANT TO GET THINGS *OFF ON THE RIGHT FOOT.* THAT IS WHAT WE HAVE JUST DONE...DEFINITELY, WE ARE OFF ON THE RIGHT FOOT!" You might also say something such as, "Doesn't it feel good to know that this program has started out right?"

Do not ignore the fact that the joke about getting things off on the right foot occurs the *third* time you ask the audience to lift up the left foot. The humor is strongest when it happens in this sequence. Comedians refer to it as the "rule of three." Because of a quirk in human nature that is hard to explain, but clearly a reality, people almost always react most strongly to something that happens in a context of three. (Think of the many ways this is evidenced...Third try is a charm, On the third strike you are out, Three Little Pigs, Three Stooges, Three Musketeers, Three wishes, etc.)

Chapter Ten: A Warm-up or Wake-up
TICKLED TO LIFE

When doing a program in Kansas City, Missouri, a pastor introduced me by saying he was "tickled to death" to have our program in his church. I had heard the expression "tickled to death" many times before, but on that occasion it lodged in my mind. I thought, "What a strange thing to say." I also thought, "I should do something fun with it."

The following bit of business is the result of that decision to turn a common saying into a useful activity.

HOW TO DO IT:

Ask the audience to stand. Also, ask them all to hold their left hand up with the palm facing downwards. Next, tell them to bring their right fingers up under the palm of their left hand and, while making a tickling motion with their fingers, say, "Tickle, tickle, tickle."

Once they have all said, "Tickle, tickle, tickle" (which is a silly event in itself that will probably cause people to laugh), say to them, "HAVE YOU EVER HEARD THE EXPRESSION 'I'M TICKLED TO DEATH?' YOU KNOW, SUCH AS 'I'M TICKLED TO DEATH TO MEET YOU' OR 'TICKLED TO DEATH THAT YOU ARE HERE'?"

Comment about the fact that it is a common expression. (You will discover, at least in the USA, that everyone has heard this expression.) Ask the audience if they have ever wondered about what it really means. Isn't the concept of death rather negative? Do we really want to have someone tell us that the prospect of meeting us has made him or her want to giggle for a while...then die?

NOW TAKE THE IDEA OF STRANGE EXPRESSIONS FURTHER...ask the audience to sing a song with you. Lead them in singing "ROCK A BYE BABY." As you lead them, stop after every line and suggest that they consider the meaning.

"Rock a bye baby, in the tree top" - Is it really a good idea to put a baby in the top of a tree?

"When the wind blows, the cradle will rock" - If the baby is up in the top of a tree, do we want the wind to be blowing?

"When the bow breaks" - Ponder that seriously. Do we actually want the branch that is holding the baby up in the top of the tree to break?

Chapter Ten: A Warm-up or Wake-up
TICKLED TO LIFE (Continued)

"The cradle will fall" - Is this a good idea? The baby is up in the top of the tree. The branch holding the baby up has broken. The baby is falling. Is this what we want to happen?

"And down will come baby, cradle and all" - Could this be a reason why our children have nightmares...because we sing them songs like this?

Of course, as you lead the song, you do it with a "tongue in cheek" or joking attitude. Most people have never thought about the meaning of the words to this lullaby. They will laugh as they discover how weird the song actually is.

After the song has been sung, say something like this: "It is too late for us to change the words to "Rock A Bye Baby." The song has been around too long. However, we can do something about the expression "Tickled To Death." Let's make it better!

Ask everyone to hold up the left hand again, with the palm down. Tell them to bring the right hand up underneath like before and say, "Tickle, tickle, tickle."

Next, tell them to raise their hands toward the sky and say with enthusiasm, the word "Hey."

Finally, tell them to combine those actions with one more thing. First, they do the "Tickle, tickle, tickle" motion. Then they lift their hands and say, "Hey" (with enthusiasm). LAST, THEY TURN TO A PERSON NEARBY AND SAY, "HEY, I AM TICKLED TO LIFE TO BE HERE TODAY, AND TICKLED TO LIFE TO BE ABLE TO SHAKE YOUR HAND."

The thrust of the gag is the concept of changing "Tickled to death" to "Tickled to life." What makes the gag a good one is the process by which you get to the change. Here is a review of the steps involved in the event.
1. Everyone stands and does the "Tickle, tickle, tickle" motion to themselves.
2. You introduce the saying, "Tickled to death." People will at least smile and maybe laugh when you suggest they ponder what it actually means.

3. You introduce another strange use of words, the song "Rock A Bye Baby." The audience is asked to join you in the song. As it is sung, a comment is made about each phrase. The result is more laughs.
4. You announce that there isn't time to change the words to "Rock A Bye Baby," but there is time to change the expression "Tickled to death." Explanation is added about how to add the motion of lifting hands and saying "Hey," to the tickle motion.
5. Everyone says, "Tickle, tickle, tickle" (while doing the tickling motion to themselves). Next, they lift their hands and say "Hey," before turning to someone to say, "Hey, I'm just tickled to life to meet you and I am tickled to life that you are here!"

Chapter Eleven: A Warm-up or Wake-up
GROUP IMPRESSIONS

This gag is especially valuable for use at retreats, camps, or extended group activities, where people are in the mood for action. It allows them to get on their feet and offers plenty of movement.

For some groups, this activity is too crazy to be appreciated. For other groups, it will be loads of fun. Use good judgment when putting it to use.

HOW TO DO IT:

Announce that it is time for some "group impressions." State, "Not only can famous comedians do impressions, you as a talented audience can do them, too!"

Ask everyone to stand for the demonstration. Instruct them to watch what you do and duplicate your motions.

Impression number one: Lift your hand above your eyes as if you are looking for something. Wait for them to do the same. Tell them, "This is an impression of a cowboy looking for his dead horse."

Drop your hand to your nose and hold your nose as if you have found something that stinks. Make sure the audience does the same. Say, "This is the cowboy finding his dead horse!"

Before doing the next few impressions, explain that you are about to imitate some well-known birds.

Impression number two: Declare that you are about to do an imitation of a duck. When everyone is watching to see what you do, just duck (bow your head and crouch down quickly).

Tell the audience they must do this. Say, "Show me your impression of a duck!" (They all duck.)

Impression number three: Tell them it is time for the impression of a swallow. Turn your head to the side and make a big gulping noise (as if you are swallowing something). This was your "swallow."

Give them a chance to do the same.

Impression number four: Ask them if they have ever seen an impression of a bat. Quickly adopt a "batting position," as if playing baseball, and act like you are "up to bat."

Again, have them all do the same.

Impression number five: This is the last impression. Present this as your big finale. Tell them, "Here it is, the impression of the great American chicken." Hold your hands up in front of you as if you are afraid and say, "Don't hurt me, don't hurt me." (You are afraid...chicken.)

Have them do this, too.

With all of the above impressions, people will laugh (or groan) when you demonstrate them. They will also laugh at themselves when they try to do them.

BUT THAT'S NOT ALL!

After all the impressions have been demonstrated and then tried by the group, ANNOUNCE THAT THERE WILL BE A TEST. You will give them a signal and state something to imitate at the same time. When this happens, they are to do the impression as quickly as possible.

THE FOLLOWING ORDER IS IMPORTANT. Years of experience have shown that this sequence gets the most laughs and works most effectively as a tool for crowd control.

1. Announce..."Cowboy looking for a dead horse...Go!" Follow this up right away by saying, "He finds it...Go!" (The audience is to adopt the position of the impression as fast as possible.)

2. Say, "Swallow...Go!"

3. Say, "Bat...Go!"

4. Say, "The great American chicken...Go!"

5. Announce, "The duck...Go!"

With this last impression, as soon as they "duck," be ready to tell them the following, "Since you are already crouching down, go ahead and slide right into your seats. Once you all are seated, give yourselves a big round of applause for putting up with all this silliness!"

Chapter Twelve: A Wake-up
"YOUR BODY IS A MACHINE!"

This is something I discovered when working with a crowd of over four hundred children. In the process of presenting a forty-minute long program to them, I realized they were losing focus on what I was doing. It may have been the temperature in the room, it may have been something else, but whatever the cause, they all seemed to have extra "wiggles" in them.

In the midst of the event, it crossed my mind that children like robots and maybe they would enjoy playing at being one. On the spot I invented the following exercise. It turned out to be especially effective. The kids liked it. It gave them an excuse to move. I remained in charge of their actions.

HOW TO DO IT:

Announce that it is time to be robots. Children will find this interesting. Explain that everyone is to do as you say and pretend that his or her body is a machine.

Tell them, "Reach up and touch your forehead. With your finger give a push. You have just turned yourself on. Hear the click?" (Make a clicking sound with your tongue. Have the children do the same.)

"You are now a machine. You can only move like a machine would move. Everything is under complete control."

Stiffly, your hand moves from your forehead back to your side.

"Feel the power in you. Slowly, you start to stand up. It is like you are made of metal. Stiffly and under control, you rise to your feet."

Once the children are on their feet, you may have them do a variety of motions. "Your hand stiffly rises up in the air. It waves back and forth at me like a robot would wave. The hand goes back down again. You turn to your side and take two long steps, like a robot would step. Then you step back again. Your head slowly turns from side to side, like a robot head would turn. Your knee rises up in the air. It seems to be stuck. It must need oil. Your other hand comes over slowly, like a robot hand, and mechanically rubs your knee. Now your knee is better. It comes back down."

After you've had some fun with this, it is time for the children to return to their seats. Do it like this, "Suddenly you feel the power begin to go away. Someone has unplugged you or else your batteries must be weak. You start to sink slowly, like a machine would sink, back into your chairs. Once you are sitting down, your hand goes up to your forehead and pushes the button again. You are completely turned off. You can breathe a big sigh of relief. You are back to normal."

When the children are back to normal, they will be ready to pay attention and you can go on with your presentation. To them, it will have been a little game. To you, it will have been a way to keep them under control.

Chapter Thirteen: A Warm-up
THE WILTING FLOWER

Many years ago, at a convention in Oklahoma, I saw someone use this technique. At the time, I did not know whose idea it actually was.

A few years later, in a booklet called "FAVORITE WARMUPS," I described the technique without giving proper credit for it.

Since then, I have learned it is the creation of Mark Wade. Mark is a terrific ventriloquist, wonderful entertainer, and busy performer on the school show circuit. I'm pleased to finally be able to put his name with the idea. Many performers are using the gag and need to know where it started. (I write about it with his permission.)

HOW TO DO IT:

A prop is required. The item is a "Wilting Flower." It can be purchased at almost any store that carries magic tricks or clown supplies.

When introduced to an audience, the performer announces he is pleased to show everyone a beautiful flower. When the flower is picked up it flops over. It has wilted. (This is a funny sight that usually gets some laughs.)

After pretending to be surprised by the turn of events, the performer turns to the audience and says, "Don't worry. This really is a beautiful flower, but it needs some encouragement. If all of the girls in this room will clap their hands, it will feel better."

The girls then applaud, but nothing happens.

"I'm surprised. I thought the girls could do it. Let's have the boys try. I'm sure if all of the boys in this room will clap their hands, the flower will perk up."

The boys applaud, but nothing happens.

"How about that? The boys couldn't do it, either. That means our only hope is cooperation. Everyone needs to work together. So everyone, clap your hands!"

Boys and girls applaud. While they do, the flower stands up. It is no longer wilted.

"Look at this! Give yourselves a big round of applause. The beautiful flower is happy again!"

This is a great warm-up because it involves a little bit of competition between boys and girls, but the winner is everyone. The victory is achieved when all work together.

It also gives the unspoken message that applause is a good thing that will be welcomed throughout the show.

Yet another benefit of this event is it can lead to comments about the value and effectiveness of cooperation.

SECTION TWO

COMEDY LINES

About The Comedy Lines

It is fun to read these lines, but their real purpose is to provide laughs for a large crowd. This means how you say the lines is important. Practice your delivery.

When looking at the longer lists of jokes, remember that it isn't necessary, or even wise, to use all of them. Select a few that you especially like. Apart from doing something similar to David Letterman's "Top Ten Lists," it is hard to get good laughs from lots of lines. Most of the time a collection of three short jokes, or from five to seven funny sayings, is plenty.

It is also necessary to consider the "set up" you will use for telling the jokes. They work better when you give some kind of reason, even if it is a silly one, for bringing up their subject.

With each list of jokes, there will be a short statement to help you establish a context for them.

HARD QUESTIONS

I once heard someone say, "About the time I think I've found the answers to life, I can't remember the questions." For those in this audience that can't remember the really hard questions of life, I will remind you of some of them.

1. When they ship Styrofoam, what do they pack it in?

2. If a man writes a book called <u>HOW TO BE A TOTAL FAILURE</u>, and no one buys the book...is it a success?

3. What do they call a coffee break at the Lipton Tea Company?

4. If a turtle were to fall out of its shell, what would it be, naked or homeless?

5. Why is abbreviated such a long word?

6. Really...what is occasional irregularity and how does it differ from regular irregularity?

7. If a person lives at the end of a one way street, how does he move?

8. Why do we call apartments "apart-ments," when actually, they are together?

9. When you see a fly on the ceiling, how did it get there? Was it flying upside down all the time, and then landed up? Or did it do a back flip at the last minute?

10. What hair color do they put on the driver's license of a bald man?

11. If every fifth child born in the world is Chinese, and you already have four children, if you have a fifth child, what language will he speak?

12. It has been said that falling bread always lands butter side up. It has been said that a falling cat will always land on his feet. What would happen if you buttered a slice of bread, strapped it on the back of a cat, and then threw the cat out the window?

IT'S A SMALL TOWN!

Does anyone here come from a small town? Maybe some of you aren't sure if your town is small or not? Here is the criteria...

1. You know it is a small town when the McDonald's restaurant only has one arch.

2. You know it is a small town when Second Street is also the city limits.

3. You know it is a small town when every time a dog crosses the street, you know its name.

4. You know it is a small town when it is necessary to widen Main Street before a yellow line can be painted down the middle.

5. You know it is small...when you get a speeding ticket and everyone in town knows about it before the patrolman gets back into his cruiser.

6. You know it is a small town when every store in town is attached to the same gas station.

7. You know it is a small town when someone plugs in his electric razor and the street lights go dim.

8. You know it is a small town when the library only has one book.

9. You know it is a small town when the zip code only has two digits.

10. You know it is a small town when the all night drug store closes at noon!

11. You know it is a small town when the mayor is also the garbage collector, school superintendent, policeman, and minister at the local church.

12. You know it is a small town when you dial the wrong number, and end up talking for 15 minutes anyway.

STRESS RELIEF

We live in tough times. A lot of people are suffering from stress. Fortunately, I recently came across some creative ways for relieving stress. I hope they help you...

1. Use your Mastercard to pay off your Visa Card. Use your Discover Card to pay off your Mastercard. Use your American Express Card to pay off your Discover Card. Then use your Visa Card to pay off your American Express Card. See how long you can get away with it!

2. Tell jokes without punch lines and watch the people who don't want you to know that they don't get it laugh anyway.

3. Put your clothes on backwards and walk around town like nothing is wrong.

4. Go shopping. Buy everything. Sweat in it. Return it the next day.

5. Bill your doctor for time spent in the waiting room.

6. Start a rumor and see if you recognize it when it comes back to you.

7. Stare at people through the tines of a fork. Pretend they are in jail. This feels especially good when you are looking at people you don't like.

8. Gently tell your dog he is an idiot and watch him wag his tail in appreciation.

9. Pretend the remote control on your television set makes people do things. Aim it at them and push the mute button.

10. Throw away your Slimfast and buy some Twinkies. If that doesn't make you feel better, nothing will!

DIETING

Have you ever wondered whether or not you should go on a diet? Have you ever wondered about the difference between being overweight or just pleasingly plump? Here is some helpful advice...

1. You know you need to diet when it rains and nothing below your waist gets wet.

2. You know you need to diet when you have a recurring nightmare about somebody named Ahab who is chasing you with a harpoon. (Don't get it? Read <u>MOBY DICK</u>.)

3. You know you need to diet when you find yourself putting a few lettuce leaves on a jumbo pizza and calling it a salad.

4. You know you need to diet when you step on your dog and it dies.

5. You know you need to diet when the couch gets up when you do.

6. You know you need to diet when, at the golf course, if you put the ball where you can hit it, you can't see it. If you put the ball where you can see it, you can't hit it.

7. You know you need to diet when your spoon needs replacement because your tongue wore a hole in it.

BORED? WHAT TO DO ABOUT IT!

In spite of the fact that ours is a busy society, sometimes people do get bored. For those who have too much time on their hands, for those who are wondering what to do when there is nothing to do, here are some ideas...

1. Call every door to door salesman you know. Tell him your neighbor is interested in his products.

2. Iron your underwear.

3. Wait for a rainy day. Take a trip to Mount Rushmore in South Dakota. See the faces of presidents carved in rock. Watch George Washington's nose run.

4. Knit a bag for your bowling ball.

5. Shave your eyebrows to see how you look.

6. Once you find out how you look, try to glue your eyebrows back on.

7. Learn all of the words to the theme song for the old Gilligan's Island T.V. show. Call up your neighbor and sing to him.

8. Follow a trail of ants to see where they go.

9. Try to get into the Guinness Book of World Records for tooth flossing. If you are successful, call up your neighbor and brag.

OLD?

When I was a child, I thought people who were forty were old. Now, I think forty looks pretty good. I'm wondering if I will ever know when I really get old. Lucky for me, I recently discovered some information that explains the matter. Here it is...

1. You know you are getting old when you start saying, "I remember when" more often than "What's new?"

2. You know you are getting old when it takes you longer to rest than it does to get tired.

3. You know you are getting old if you can remember when the Big Dipper was only a drinking cup.

4. You know you are getting old when you know what L.S.M.F.T. means. (Lucky Strike Means Fine Tobacco - it's an old commercial.)

5. You know you are getting old when you can remember the first time the outfit you just bought was in style.

6. You know you are getting old when everything hurts. If it doesn't hurt, it doesn't work.

7. You know you are getting old when you can't wait for Baskin-Robbins to come out with Oat Bran-flavored ice cream.

8. You know you are getting old when you know all the answers to questions nobody is asking.

9. You know you are getting old when your knees buckle, but your belt won't.

10. You know you are getting old when you sit in a rocking chair and can't get it going.

11. You know you are getting old when you sink your teeth into a big steak and they stay there.

12. You know you are getting old when you have too much room in the house and not enough room in the medicine chest.

A REAL DAD

Some say fatherhood is a lost art. I disagree. There are plenty of real dads around today. Here is how you know when you see one...

1. Real dads keep their pencils in a can decorated with gold sprayed macaroni. (Real dads know about this.)

2. Real dads have played "CANDYLAND" more than once.

3. Real dads know what "CANDYLAND" is! (It's a board game.)

4. Real dads stick out from under cars they repair, while a child holding a wrench watches.

5. Real dads hold onto a teddy bear while a child gets a toy from the vending machine.

6. Real dads reach under the vending machine to retrieve the toy that gets dropped by a child, while the child holds the teddy bear.

7. Real dads listen to knock knock jokes.

8. Real dads walk stiff legged, with children sitting on their shoes, to create a fun ride.

9. Real dads let children sit on their necks at parades.

10. Real dads offer to help with science projects and end up doing the whole thing.

11. Real dads never eat the last cookie, unless it is homemade chocolate chip and a real mom has hidden it for him behind some dusty glasses on the top shelf.

CAN YOU BELIEVE IT?

Have you ever heard someone say, "I can't believe it?" Usually, I can believe it. Yet, sometimes, people tell me things that are hard to believe. For example...

1. "The check is in the mail."

2. "I'm from the government and I'm here to help."

3. "Go ahead and tell me. I promise I won't get mad."

4. "This car is just like brand new. It was owned by a retired schoolteacher who never went anywhere."

5. "There is no need to put it in writing. You have my personal guarantee."

6. When it says on a postcard, "Wish you were here!"

7. When a parent says, "You made that all by yourself? I never would have known!"

8. When a husband says, "Put away the map, dear; I know exactly where we are."

9. When a child says, "I promise. If you get me a puppy it won't be any trouble. I will do all the work to take care of it!"

10. When a teen-ager says, "May I use the phone? It will only take a second."

11. When the gossipy neighbor says, "I can only stay and talk a minute."

12. When the mechanic says, "Don't worry, it will be ready by five o'clock."

13. When the doctor says, "It won't hurt a bit."

14. When the husband says, "I am not putting golf before my family. I promise that next weekend I'll clean the garage and do anything else you want around the house."

15. The ad that says, "Lose ten pounds a week without dieting."

DUMBBELLS

Exercise in stupidity creates dumbbells. How do you know if a dumbbell has been created? Consider these observations...

1. A dumbbell is someone who must never stop to think, for he may not get started again.

2. A dumbbell is someone who needs an hour and a half to cook "minute rice."

3. A dumbbell is someone who goes to the Zoo to see what Easter Seals look like.

4. A dumbbell is someone who stands in front of a mirror with his eyes shut, trying to figure out what he looks like when asleep.

5. A dumbbell is someone who stands in front of a mirror for a long time...trying to figure out where he has seen himself before.

6. A dumbbell is someone who takes a memory course and memorizes one hundred phone numbers, but fails to memorize any of the names that go with them.

BIG HEAD

I have a friend. I won't say he brags a lot. But, I will say...

1. Every time he opens his mouth he puts his "feats" in.

2. He is easily entertained. All he has to do is listen to himself talk.

3. He is a self-made man who insists on giving everyone the recipe.

4. He tries to push himself ahead by patting himself on the back.

5. You could make a fortune off of him, if you could buy him for what you think of him, and then sell him for what he thinks of himself.

6. Every time he looks into a mirror, he takes a bow.

7. When someone says to him, "You are brilliant!" He says, "I'll bet you say that to everyone who is brilliant."

8. He is a boss you can't help but admire. If you don't, you are fired!

WHY KEEP IT?

Any packrats here? Can any of you relate to saving things that others think should be thrown out? If you are such a person, you have your reasons. Here are some of them...

1. Why do I keep that old Christmas wrapping paper? Because I can iron it and use it one more time!

2. Why do I save that broken watch? Because I might need to use its crystal as a magnifying glass in a survival situation!

3. Why keep expired stacks of grocery coupons? They represent such a good deal!

4. Why keep ball point pens that don't write anymore? What if I found some cheap refills? Then I could use them again!

5. Why keep that pair of pantyhose with the 2" wide runner up the back? If I wear them under jeans, no one will notice!

6. Why do I keep those half read books that I couldn't force myself to finish? If I ever get jailed, snowed in, or hospitalized, I might finish them, after all!

7. Why keep lidless cookie jars? Throwing innocent objects like that into the garbage seems merely a step away from murder!

8. Why do I keep that rusted out car in my yard? What if I need it for spare parts!

9. Why do I keep that pair of pants that I can't fit into anymore and I haven't worn once in three years, anyway? Because they are still perfectly good. There is nothing wrong with them!

10. Why do I keep all that stuff in my garage that makes it impossible to park my car inside? Because someday I am going to go through it all!

11. Why do I save that thing that they don't make anymore? Because they don't make it anymore! (Why is it that they don't make it anymore?)

12. Why do I save those broken appliances? Because they will give me something to work on when a rainy day comes! (Do you really want to work on broken appliances on a rainy day?)

A BAD DAY WHEN...

Ever think you are having a bad day? Maybe you have, maybe you haven't. Here is how to be sure...

1. You know you are having a bad day when the pilot of your DC 10 interrupts the mid-flight movie and asks to borrow duct tape.

2. You know you are having a bad day when the man you just hired to remodel your summer home appears in the local post office on one of the wanted posters.

3. You know you are having a bad day when the engine of your car starts making odd whining noises and you realize your cat is missing.

4. You know you are having a bad day when the man who owns the motorcycle that you just bumped over out in the parking lot has tattoos on his tongue.

5. You know you are having a bad day when you page through your child's easy reader and can't do the word search.

6. You know you are having a bad day when you stand up and realize that you still have a lap.

7. You know you are having a bad day when you put your clothes on backwards...and they fit better!

LATE

Here are some real excuses for being late. They were submitted as part of a contest sponsored by a newspaper in Michigan. The time may come when you need to use one of them...

1. I was late for work because someone stole one of my shoes while I was riding the bus.

2. I was late for work because a band of Greenpeace fanatics was blocking the road to protest international whaling. Traffic was backed up for miles.

3. I was late to school because my tongue got stuck to a metal pole in cold weather and my mom didn't notice me not getting on the bus.

4. I was late to work because a spider held me captive in the bathroom. (Submitted by a woman with a phobia about spiders.)

5. I was late to work because my garbage was stolen. I had to drive around the neighborhood looking for it. (If they stole my garbage, I'd let them have it!)

6. I was late to work because I ate so much during vacation that none of my clothes would fit, and I had to spend the morning getting them altered.

7. I was late to work because I spotted what looked like a flying saucer, and followed it on the highway for fifty miles. I still didn't figure out what it was.

8. I was late to work because my pig fell into the furnace and I had to spend the morning getting it out. (A true story - The man had a small farm. One of his pet pigs got sick, so he brought it into the house to watch overnight. He was in the process of remodeling his home and had the heat registers removed from the furnace ducts. During the night, the pig started feeling better, so got up to walk around. It fell into an open duct. The pig squealed and snorted as it slid into the furnace. Fortunately the furnace wasn't on, so the pig didn't become pork.)

EXCUSES

When you are late or absent, you need a good excuse. Here are some real excuses, submitted by parents, to explain a situation with their child. (The spelling mistakes and improper usage of words are theirs.)

1. My son is under the doctor's care. Please execute him.

2. Please excuse my daughter for being absent. She is sick and I had her shot.

3. Please excuse my son, Fred, for being. It was his father's fault.

4. Please excuse my son for being absent on January 28, 29, 30, 31, 32, 33.

5. My son had to stay home from school today because he has an acre in his side.

6. Please excuse my son from P.E. class for a few days. He fell yesterday out of a tree and misplaced his hip.

BUDGET

Let's talk about money! Actually, let's talk about the aspect of money that most of us aren't very good at. Saving it...

1. A budget is saving quarters in a glass jar for next Christmas, and then spending them by Easter.

2. A budget is spending 15 dollars on gas to drive to a special shopping mall, where you save 4 dollars and 30 cents on a 20-pound turkey.

3. About balancing a budget...why should you have to do it when the government can't?

4. A budget is a plan that falls apart when the plumber makes an emergency visit.

5. A budget is trying to figure out how the family next door is doing it.

6. A budget is when you buy a designer coat on the same day you purchased day old bread.

7. A budget is trying to make 25 dollars go as far today as when you were first married.

8. A budget is when you are in a store and find a dress that is two sizes too small, but go ahead and purchase it anyway, because it is such a good deal.

9. Money may not make the world go around, but if you don't have it, your world tends to come to a screeching halt.

10. Money isn't everything, but without it you can't get much of anything.

USELESS INFORMATION

Someone has said that it is good to listen to counsel and good to get advice. Here is some advice that I'm not sure has helped me much...

1. Chances are, if your grandparents never had any children, you won't either.

2. Never put off until tomorrow what you can get someone else to do for you today.

3. A day without junk food is like a day without sunshine.

4. Keep smiling, it makes people wonder what you have been up to.

5. Never kiss someone on an empty stomach. Behind the ears or on the hands, but never on an empty stomach.

6. Never make the same mistakes twice, go ahead...make new ones!

7. If you could remove the rim from a zero, you would accomplish nothing.

8. Don't let the light of your life be a light bulb in a refrigerator.

9. Don't go to a doctor whose office plants are dead.

10. If at first you don't succeed, don't take up sky diving.

11. If you don't have something good to say about somebody, go on an afternoon talk show and say it anyway.

12. Never trust a surgeon who already has three Band-Aids on his fingers.

13. Sometimes stretch-pants have no other choice.

14. Don't forget, eagles may fly, but weasels don't get stuck in jet engines.

15. A flea circus may be a good act, but if you really want to bring down the house, use termites.

16. Life definitely is not fair. Proof? A girl's best friend is a diamond. A man's best friend is a dog.

17. If each and every car in America was lined up end for end, some fool would pull out and try to pass them all.

18. If you hold your chin up, put your shoulder to the wheel, and nose to the grindstone, you may become a success...but you will look really stupid.

19. If all of the joggers on Planet Earth were laid end for end, 71% of them would drown.

20. Show me a man who has both feet firmly planted on this earth, and I'll show you a man who has a tough time changing his trousers!

21. Don't buy hair restorer from a bald man. (Actually, this may be good advice,)

ANOTHER WAY TO SAY CRAZY

Do you know anybody that is crazy? Do you know anyone to whom some of the following terms might apply?

1. A few french fries short of a Happy Meal.

2. The tacos have fallen off his combination plate.

3. The lights are on, but no one is home.

4. His train has jumped the track.

5. The wheel is spinning, but the hamster is dead.

6. A few sandwiches short of a picnic.

7. Someone is standing on his air hose.

8. The elevator doesn't reach the top floor.

9. There is ketchup on his shoelaces and bow knots in his french fries.

10. The wheels fell off of his tricycle.

11. He has screen doors on his submarine.

12. The helicopter on his beanie doesn't make complete circles.

13. The fixture is wired, but the bulb is dim.

14. There are no clowns in his circus.

15. Too much yardage between the goalposts.

16. To have a deep thought he needs a ride in a submarine.

17. There is a town named after him...it is Marblehead, Massachusetts.

18. Why does he keep his head above water? Wood floats!

19. If she gets a phone call while ironing, she will burn her ear!

20. The wheels on his shopping cart don't all turn the same direction.

POSITIVE THINKING

Everyone says it is important to be a positive thinker. They say that to be a success one must be a positive thinker. I want to be a success, so I wanted to know how to identify a positive thinker. Here is what I learned...

1. A positive thinker is someone who falls from the top of a twenty-story building, and on the way down says, "So far so good!" as he passes the window at the thirteenth floor.

2. A positive thinker is someone who notices his clothes are getting too tight and blames it on the dry cleaners.

3. A positive thinker is someone who takes a frying pan and camera along when he goes fishing.

4. A positive thinker is a man who goes into a restaurant without any money, because he expects to pay for his meal with the pearl he will find in the oyster stew.

5. A positive thinker is a boss who marries his secretary and thinks he is still going to dictate to her.

6. A positive thinker is a mother who believes it when her child says, "If you get me that new puppy, I will do all of the work to take care of it!"

7. A positive thinker is a husband who says to his wife, "Put away the map, dear; I know exactly where we are!"

The story is told of a boy who came home from school with a sad expression on his face. To his father he said, "I think I flunked my math test today."
His father said, "Son, in our family we are positive thinkers. I don't like how your statement sounded. Try it again."
The boy said, "OK, I am positive I flunked my math test today."

NEGATIVE THINKING

Have you ever suffered from "stinking thinking?" It is also sometimes called "hardening of the attitudes." Here is your chance to check yourself out on the matter. Listen to these descriptions of a pessimist...

1. A pessimist is someone who manages to always find at least a little bit of bad in the best of things.

2. A pessimist is someone who, when told that life begins at forty, says, "So does rheumatism!"

3. A pessimist is someone who never worries about tomorrow; he already knows everything will turn out wrong.

4. A pessimist is someone who doesn't like flowers...they remind him of funerals.

5. A pessimist is someone who, when told that "O" is the first letter in opportunity, responds by saying, "It is also the last letter in zero!"

6. A pessimist is one who is always pulling tomorrow's clouds over today's sunshine.

LOSING WEIGHT

Here is something most people want to know - how to lose weight! I've got some dieting secrets to share...

1. Find new ways to burn calories such as setting fire to a pan of brownies.

2. Don't reward yourself for only eating two meals a day by eating three meals a night.

3. Avoid Dr. Waddle's fudge diet.

4. Secure your refrigerator with a two-hundred number combination lock.

5. Eat all you want. Just make sure you never want much.

6. Use cookbooks written in a language you can't read.

7. Eat nothing but broth, and use a fork.

8. Never eat anything on an empty stomach.

IS YOUR MARRIAGE IN TROUBLE?

If you are wondering about the strength of your marriage, here are some points to ponder...

1. Ladies, you know your marriage is in trouble when your husband stops saying, "My little chickadee," and starts saying, "Dumb cluck."

2. Men, you know your marriage is in trouble when the only time your wife takes her arms and puts them around your neck is when she is looking for ring around the collar.

3. Husbands and wives, you know your marriage is in trouble when the last time the two of you had a candlelight dinner was when the electricity went off, and you shared a can of tuna.

4. Husbands and wives, you know your marriage is in trouble when the most romantic movie the two of you have seen in years is a rerun of "Son Of Flubber."

5. Husbands and wives, you know your marriage is in trouble when the money you were saving for that romantic getaway is spent on new sprinkler heads for the lawn, and neither of you cares.

6. Husbands and wives, you know your marriage is in trouble when the most meaningful conversation that takes place between the two of you at the dinner table is when one says to the other, "Please pass the meatloaf."

HEAVEN?

A survey was done with a group of grade school students. They were asked what they thought about heaven. Their answers were surprising and original.

1. A little boy said, "God doesn't tell you when you are going to die, because He wants it to be a big surprise."

2. Another boy said, "When you die, God takes care of you like your mother did when you were alive, only He doesn't yell at you all the time."

3. A girl said, "I sure hope I die when I am sound asleep. That way I won't bother anybody."

4. Another girl said, "I hope I don't die with my brother, because I don't want him to sock me in heaven, too."

5. Another girl said, "Only good people go to heaven. Other people have to go where it is hot, like Florida!"

6. Another boy said, "Doctors help you so you won't die until after you pay your bills."

7. A girl said, "When you die, they put you in a box and bury you in the ground, because you don't look too good."

MORON JOKES

I suppose they aren't "politically correct" now, but I still remember the "moron" jokes my friends and I would tell when I was young. Maybe some of you told them, too. Remember any of these...

1. Why did the moron throw the clock out the window? He wanted to see time fly!

2. Why did the moron shoot his alarm clock with a shotgun? He was just trying to kill time.

3. Why did the moron tiptoe past the medicine cabinet? He didn't want to wake up the sleeping pills.

4. Why did the moron feed cough syrup to the pony? It was feeling a little hoarse.

5. Why did the moron race round and round his bed as fast as he could? He was trying to catch up on his sleep.

6. Why did the moron say he could never be a pharmacist? He didn't know how to get those little bottles into his typewriter.

I suppose blonde jokes also aren't politically correct. Nevertheless, I will comment that "blonde" would work in the above lines instead of "moron."

A WIMP

What exactly is a wimp? Ever wonder about it? Here are some answers...

1. A wimp is a man who lives in constant fear that his last breath will be a burp, and he won't have the opportunity to say, "Excuse me."

2. A wimp is a man who won't open an oyster without first knocking politely on the shell.

3. A wimp is a man who can only be decisive in one situation. It is when he gives a "definite maybe."

4. A wimp is a man who is told by his psychiatrist, "No, you don't have an inferiority complex. You are inferior!"

5. A wimp is a man who is so timid he tells an elevator operator, "I would like to go to the twenty-second floor, please. That is, if it isn't out of your way."

6. A wimp is a man so indecisive he has a seven-year-old son that he hasn't named yet!

HEN-PECKED OR ROOSTER-BITTEN?

Are you married and do you feel picked on? Do you have a right to feel picked on? Here is how you can know for sure...

1. Husbands, you know you are hen-pecked when you always get the last words and they are "I apologize."

2. Husbands, you know you are hen-pecked when you find yourself spending the evening solving crossword puzzles, and your wife is the one who supplies the crosswords.

3. Husbands, you know you are hen-pecked when the only time your wife runs her fingers through your hair is when she can't find a towel.

4. Husbands, you know you are hen-pecked when your wife asks you what you would like for dinner, and then tells you the restaurant where you can get it.

5. Wives, you know you are rooster-bitten when your husband tells you that you are the driving force in the household, and then gives you a hammer and nails while pointing at pictures that need to be hung.

6. Wives, you know you are rooster-bitten when your husband forgets your birthday, but remembers your age.

7. Wives, you know you are rooster-bitten when you tell your husband he is a cross, ill-mannered, inconsiderate brute, and he says, "Look, honey, nobody is perfect!"

8. Wives, you know you are rooster-bitten when your husband puts you up on a pedestal and says, "Now, can you reach the ceiling with your paint roller?"

LOVE IS

True love is a wonderful thing. Here are the signs of its reality...

1. Love is telling her yes, when you would rather say no.
2. Love is apologizing even when you know you are right.
3. Love is moving her furniture...again.
4. Love is letting him keep that junk...that should have been thrown out long ago.
5. Love is waiting an hour because she says, "Just a minute."
6. Love is looking the other way when she weighs herself.
7. Love is listening to his problems when you have plenty of your own.
8. Love is kissing her before you ask, "What's for dinner?"
9. Love is letting him keep his fish bait in the refrigerator.
10. Love is laughing at her joke...when she told it all wrong.

COUNTRY SONGS

Looking for deep and meaningful music? Nobody can touch your heart like a country-western singer. As proof, here are some real titles to actual country songs...

1. "I Sometimes Feel Like A Bug On The Windshield of Life."

2. "We Live In A Two Story House. She's Got Her Story And I've Got Mine."

3. "My Wife Just Left With My Best Friend And I Sure Do Miss Him."

4. "For Better Or Worse But Not For Long."

5. "I'm So Miserable Without You It Is Almost Like You Are Here."

6. "The Worst You Ever Gave Me Was The Best I Ever Had."

7. "Our Marriage Was A Failure, But Our Divorce Ain't Working Either."

8. "You Took My Heart And Stomped It Flat."

THINGS NOT TO DO

Many people have "To Do" lists. Have you ever considered the value of having a "Not To Do" list? Here are some things I have put on mine...

1. Do not lick the blades of a blender while they are still turning.

2. Do not use the bottom stall in a two story outhouse.

3. Do not sniff the inside of bowling shoes.

4. Do not try to milk a wolverine.

5. Do not let Zorro autograph the back of the shirt you are wearing.

6. Do not take a memory course from a man who has his shirt on backwards.

7. Do not keep your pet snake in the same cage where you have your baby chicken.

8. Do not eat oysters, sauerkraut, rutabagas, and liver casserole more than two days in a row.

9. Do not drop out of school, especially if your class is on the fourteenth floor.

10. Never ever, ever, ever, ever, ever, ever, ever, ever repeat yourself. Never ever, ever, ever, ever, ever, ever, ever repeat yourself.

WORLD'S SHORTEST BOOKS

Busy people don't have time to read long books. Here is a collection of the top ten shortest books in the world. Read them when you have time...

10. The Plumber's Guide to Dressing Fancy

9. Dr. Kevorkian's Collection of Motivational Speeches

8. Things I Would Not Do for Money - By Dennis Rodman

7. Letting Loose the Wild and Exciting Side of Your Personality - By Former Vice-President Al Gore

6. The Encyclopedia of America's Popular Lawyers

5. Mike Tyson's Guide to Dating Success

4. Different Ways to Spell Bob

3. The Amish Phone Directory

2. Everything Women Know About Men

1. Everything Men Know About Women

Here are some more that you may want to add to the list:
- Belch Your Way to Success
- Bill Clinton's Book of Virtues
- The Masked Magician's Guide to Long Term Career Success
- Perfect Men That I Have Known

LIGHT BULBS

I've done some research that might interest you. I've investigated the matter of "changing the light bulb" and learned that almost everyone does it differently. Here's what I mean...

1. How many government employees does it take to change a light bulb? Forty-five. One to change it. Forty-four to do the paperwork.

2. How many lawyers does it take to change a light bulb? How many can you afford?

3. How many policemen does it take to change a light bulb? None. It turned itself in.

4. How many graduate students does it take to change a light bulb? Only one, but he will need five years to get it done.

5. How many country singers does it take to change a light bulb? Five. One to change it, four to sing songs about how much they miss the old one.

6. How many auto mechanics does it take to change a light bulb? Five. One to remove the old one from the socket. One to force the new one into the socket with a hammer. Three to go get spare parts.

7. How many politicians does it take to change a light bulb? Seventeen. The breakdown is as follows: One will assure everyone that the light bulb is being changed properly. While he does so, another one will twist the light bulb into the end of a water faucet. While those two do that, the other fifteen will testify before various committees that they had nothing to do with the changing of the light bulb, but, nevertheless, request a fifteen million dollar appropriation to investigate the matter.

8. How many teamsters does it take to change a light bulb? Fourteen. You got a problem with that?

9. How many chiropractors does it take to change a light bulb? Only one, but to get the job done he will need to make thirty weekly visits.

NOTE: This next one is an "inside" type joke. Professional magicians will get it. The average reader probably will be "in the dark."

10. How many magicians does it take to change a light bulb? Nine thousand, nine hundred, ninety-nine. The breakdown is as follows: One to change it. One to write the review for *MAGIC* magazine. Two to debate whether the method used is Marlo or Vernon. Ninety-five to tell how they would improve the methods of Marlo and Vernon. Two hundred to criticize the review as it will appear in *MAGIC* magazine. Two hundred more to write letters that disagree with the first two hundred critics. Three thousand one hundred forty six to say they thought of changing the light bulb first, and therefore, should get credit for the idea. Six thousand three hundred twenty-two to take the changing of the light bulb and add it to their own acts!

11. How many Southern Baptists does it take to change a light bulb? Fifteen million...if you can get them to agree that it needs to be changed.

12. How many Methodists does it take to change a light bulb? We aren't sure, but they are doing a study on the matter and there will be a report at the next annual convention.

13. How many Nazarenes does it take to change a light bulb? Eleven. One to change it, ten to organize the fellowship supper that follows.

14. How many Catholics does it take to change a light bulb? Three. One to change it. One to raffle off the old one. One to shout "Bingo" when it is done.

15. How many Charismatics does it take to change a light bulb? Three. One to change it, two to rebuke the powers of darkness.

16. How many Presbyterians does it take to change a light bulb? None. They never change anything.

LIGHT BULBS (Continued)

17. How many Californians does it take to change a light bulb? Five. One to change it, while four more sit in a hot tub and discuss the environmental impact.

18. How many mystery writers does it take to change a light bulb? Only one, but you can be sure he will give it a surprising twist!

19. How many pit bulls does it take to change a light bulb? We don't know. When we asked him to try he walked over, lifted his leg on the ladder, and walked away.

20. How many poodles does it take to change a light bulb? We don't know this, either. They wiggle their rear ends so much; they keep falling off the ladder.

21. How many bull dogs does it take to change a light bulb? We don't know. We did get one to crawl up the ladder and latch on to the light bulb, but now he won't let go. He is still hanging there.

22. How many golden retrievers does it take to change a light bulb? Only one, but he keeps bringing the old one back again.

23. How many Dobermans does it take to change a light bulb? Only one, but be prepared, you've got to let him eat the old one.

24. How many beagles does it take to change a light bulb? Are you kidding? The sun is shining, the day is young, his whole life is before him, do you really think he is going to stop and change a light bulb?

25. How many cats does it take to change a light bulb? There is not a cat on the planet who cares enough to stop and give it a try!

THE CHICKEN CROSSED THE ROAD

You probably have an answer to the question, "Why did the chicken cross the road?" but do you know how famous people would answer the question? I've done some research and learned what a few of them would say...

1. Captain James T. Kirk - "To boldly go where no chicken has gone before!"

2. Shirley McClain - "Because in its previous life as a possum it was something it could never actually do!"

3. Rush Limbaugh - "Obviously because of a liberal left-wing plot!"

4. Martin Luther King - "Because it had a dream."

5. Howard Cosell - "It may very well have been one of the most astonishing events in the annals of history. To think that an avian biped would have the temerity to attempt such an unprecedented feat and Herculean achievement is truly a cause for wonder, respect, and admiration!"

6. Bob Dylan - "How many roads must one chicken cross?"

7. Bill Clinton - "I want you to look at me...that chicken did not cross the road. One foot did move in front of the other to propel it across the pavement, but in my definition, that is not crossing the road!"

STUPID WARNINGS

The following warnings actually appeared on products sold in the USA. Don't you wish you paid more attention to such things?

1. On NYTOL sleep aid: Warning, this product may cause drowsiness. (Wow, what a surprise!)

2. On a string of Christmas lights, made in China, but sold in the USA: Warning, this product for indoor or outdoor use only! (Isn't that helpful? Otherwise, some fool would have tried to use them somewhere else!)

3. On a food processor, made in Japan, but sold in the USA: Warning, this product is not to be used for the other use. (Don't you wonder what the other use is?)

4. On a packet of nuts handed out on an American Airlines flight: Instructions, open packet and eat nuts. (Who would have thought of that?)

5. On the box containing a Rowenta clothes iron: Warning, do not iron clothes on body. (Actually, that it is a necessary warning. A number of people, to save time, have tried to do this and been burned!!)

6. On a chainsaw, made in Sweden, sold in the USA: Warning, do not attempt to stop the chain with your hands. (There's some advice we all need!)

7. On a child's Superman costume: Caution, wearing this garment does not enable wearer to fly! (What a disappointment!)

DEFINITIONS

Word meanings change as times change. It is important to stay up to date about such things, so here are some of the latest definitions to common terms...

1. Gentleman - A man who holds the door open for his wife, while she carries in the groceries.

2. Satisfaction - The feeling you get when you see the person who cut you off at the bypass doing eighty miles an hour...pulled over by the highway patrol four miles on down the road.

3. Loser - A man who can't win at Bingo even when he is the only one playing the game.

4. Diet Coke - A beverage to purchase at a convenience store at the same time you buy a box of "Ho Ho's" and a pound of peanut M&M's.

5. Pull - What the sign on the door will always say when your arms are full of boxes.

6. Celebrity - A person who works hard to become well-known and famous, then wears dark glasses to keep from being recognized.

7. Bacteria - The back room of a cafeteria.

8. Patience - What people think you have when actually you just can't decide what to do.

9. Dentist - Someone who sticks two instruments and his hand into your mouth, and then expects you to answer his questions.

10. Minor Operation - Surgery performed on anyone but you.

11. Politician - One who has what it takes to takes what you has. (Actually, that definition is nothing new!)

12. Denial - A river in Egypt.

13. Senile - A reason to go to Egypt.

14. Warehouse - Cry of a person lost in a blizzard.

15. Wedding ring - World's smallest handcuff.

16. Politics - When a parrot swallows a watch.

17. Nitrate - Lower than the day rate.

THINGS LAWYERS HAVE SAID

Here are some actual words from the mouths of those whom we trust to defend us in court...

1. Now, doctor, isn't it true that when a person dies in his sleep, he doesn't know about it until the next morning?

2. Your youngest son, the twenty-year-old, how old is he?

3. Were you present when your picture was taken?

4. Was it you or your younger brother that was killed in the car?

5. Did he kill you?

6. How far apart were the two vehicles at the time of the collision?

7. How many times have you committed suicide?

8. So you were there until you left...is that true?

9. So the date of the conception of the baby was August eighth?
   - Yes.
   - And what were you doing at the time?

10. She had three children, right?
    - Yes.
    - And how many were boys?
    - None.
    - And how many were girls?

11. You say the stairs went down to the basement?
    - Yes.
    - And these stairs, did they go up, also?

12. This Myasthenia Gravis, does it affect your memory at all?
    - Yes.
    - In what ways does it affect your memory?
    - I forget.
    - You forget? Can you give us an example of something you have forgotten?

THINGS WITNESSES HAVE SAID

Witnesses don't always help us get to the truth. Here are some actual words of testimony that have been given in court, under oath...

1. How old is your son, the one living with you?
   - Thirty-eight or thirty-nine, I can't remember which.
   - And how long has this son been living with you?
   - Forty-five years!

2. What was the first thing your husband said to you when he woke that morning?
   - He said, "Where am I, Cathy?"
   - And why did that upset you?
   - My name is Susan.

3. Did you blow your horn or anything before the accident?
   - Sure, I played for ten years. I even went to school for it.

4. Do you know if your daughter has ever been involved in voodoo or the occult?
   - We both do.
   - Voodoo?
   - We do.
   - You do?
   - Voodoo.

FOR MAGICIANS

Since the author's profession is that of magician, he shares the following help for those in his line of work... (Mainly "inside" jokes)

1. You know you are a magician when someone asks for a piece of rope and you "just happen" to have one in your pocket.

2. You know you are a magician when you want a coin in your left hand, but to get it there, must first pick it up with the right hand.

3. You know you are a magician when you pay sixty-five dollars for a book, get only two useful ideas from it, and think it is a good deal.

4. You know you are a magician when you actually do have a use for rubber cement.

5. You know you are a magician when you are careful not to accidentally spend some of the change you carry around in your pocket.

6. You know you are a magician when anytime you are seated at a table you find yourself thinking, "What would those cups look like upside down?"

7. You know you are a magician when you have boxes full of lecture notes you have never read, but still are excited about going out and buying more.

8. You know you are a magician when you do not think of a shell as something found at a beach.

9. You know you are a magician when you actually like it when you get a fifty cent piece as change.

10. You know you are a magician when all of your friends have names that start with "The Amazing" or "The Great."

11. You know you are a magician when you palm a movie ticket, pretend to have misplaced it, then as the ticket taker watches, casually produce it out of "thin air."

FOUL (FOWL) HUMOR

Here are some jokes that are "for the birds"...

1. What do you get when it rains chickens and ducks? Foul weather.

2. Why did the duck go to the doctor? His lips were quacked.

3. Why do people cut the heads off of turkeys before they roast them? Because a mind is a terrible thing to baste.

4. What do you get when you cross a rooster with a duck? A chicken that wakes you up at the quack of dawn.

5. What kind of birds are most religious? Birds of prey.

6. What do you get when you cross two canaries with a pair of roller skates? Cheap skates.

7. What do you call a parakeet wearing a raincoat? Poly unsaturated.

8. Hear about the computer dating agency for chickens? It went bankrupt; they couldn't make hens meet.

THE SOUTH

If you aren't from the South, here are some things you need to know...

1. If someone says he is "fixing to do" something, it doesn't mean anything is broken.

2. Don't be surprised to find movie rentals and bait in the same store.

3. Get used to the statement, "It's not the heat, it's the humidity." It often will be followed by, "Call this hot? Wait till August!"

4. Remember, a Mercedes Benz is not a status symbol. A Ford F-150 is.

5. If someone says, "These peppers ain't hot!" - they are.

6. Barbecue is a food group. It doesn't mean grilling hamburgers or steaks. You eat it. "I'll have a barbecue!"

7. Everything goes better with ranch dressing. Don't question it, just accept it. (If you are in the Deep South, everything goes better with Tabasco.)

8. You can say anything you want about anybody as long as you preface it with, "Bless his heart." "Bless his heart, he's a jerk!" "Bless her heart, she's a loser."

TOP TEN REASONS A MAGICIAN SHOULD BE PRESIDENT

   Here's something to remember when voting time comes around; magicians make good presidents. Here are the top ten reasons why...

10. Will bring his own rabbit to the White House Easter egg hunt.

9. Saws people in half without cutting Social Security benefits.

8. When he borrows money, after he folds, spindles, and mutilates it, he still eventually gives it back.

7. He floats people in the air without raising taxes.

6. Uses magic wands, not nuclear warheads.

5. Can produce money out of thin air.

4. Has nothing up his sleeve but flowers.

3. Links rings but doesn't get linked with scandals.

2. Does tricks with cards, but doesn't play games with the national debt.

1. People already expect him to say one thing, but do another!

TOP TEN REASONS A CLOWN SHOULD BE PRESIDENT

If you can't vote for a magician, how about a clown? Here is what one has to offer...

10. Juggles red rubber balls, not financial records.

9. Might use those big shoes to stamp out crime.

8. Wears a big wig, but doesn't act like one.

7. Uses rubber chicken, not an AK47.

6. Might use big red nose to sniff out corruption in high places.

5. Can be trusted to be funny, but doesn't do funny things with your trust.

4. Knows the difference between telling a joke and being one.

3. Is an expert on the inflation of balloons, but doesn't inflate the economy.

2. Wears make-up, but doesn't make up stories to deceive the public.

1. Will fit right in with all the other clowns who have already been elected!

WHAT I LEARNED FROM MOM

It is amazing how a mother can impart deep and wonderful truths to a child. Here are some things I learned from her while very young...

1. To appreciate - She said, "If you are going to kill each other, do it outside! I just finished cleaning the house."

2. About religion - She said, "You had better pray that comes out of the carpet."

3. About time travel - She said, "If you don't straighten up, I'll knock you into the middle of next week!"

4. About osmosis - She said, "Shut your mouth and eat your supper."

5. About contortionism - She said, "Will you just look at the dirt in your ears!"

6. About verbal accuracy - She said, "If I've told you once, I've told you a million times, don't exaggerate!"

7. About the circle of life - She said, "I brought you into this world and I can take you out!"

THE DOCTOR KNOWS

Here are some actual notes from doctors' charts. They are definitely clever professionals!

1. The patient has chest pain if she lies on her side for over a year.

2. On the second day the knee got better. On the third day it completely disappeared.

3. The patient has been depressed ever since she began seeing me in 1993.

4. The patient is tearful and crying constantly. She also appears to be depressed.

5. Discharge status: Alive, but without permission.

6. This healthy-appearing, decrepit sixty-nine-year-old male is mentally alert, but forgetful.

7. The patient refused an autopsy.

8. The patient has no history of past suicides.

A FEW JOKES FOR VARIOUS CATEGORIES

Here is a variety of themes, followed by a short series of jokes that relate to it.

MARRIAGE

1. Good marriages are made in heaven. So is lightning and thunder.

2. Our marriage is a 50/50 relationship. Half the time my wife is right, and the other half of the time I am wrong.

3. We have a wonderful give and take relationship. I give her what she wants, or she takes it.

4. She is the woman who cuts my sorrow in half, makes my joy double, and my expenses triple.

5. People wonder how we met...it was at a travel agency. She was looking for a vacation and I was the last resort.

COWS

1. What do you call the winner of a cow beauty contest? The dairy queen.

2. Where do cows go for vacation? Some say "Cow-lorado," but I think it is "Moo-souri."

3. What do you call a female cow who lives at a dairy, but can't give milk? An udder failure.

4. What is a cow's favorite love song? "If Heifer I Would Leave You."

5. What do you get when you milk an absent-minded cow? Milk of amnesia.

6. What do cows like to do when they relax? Listen to Moo-sic.

SKUNKS

1. What happened to the skunk that couldn't swim when it fell into the ocean? It stank right to the bottom.

2. What do you get when you cross a skunk with a boomerang? A smell that won't go away.

3. What do you get when you cross a skunk with a cute little orange bear? Winnie the phew!

4. What kind of book do skunks hope to write? A best smeller.

RABBITS

1. What do you call a rabbit with fleas? Bugs bunny.

2. What happens when a rabbit loses his tail? He goes to a retail store to get a new one.

3. What did the rabbit say when his true love left him? Nothing, but he was very un-hoppy.

4. What do you call a wealthy rabbit? A million-hare.

5. What is the theme song for a rabbit wedding? Hare comes the bride.

6. Where do you take a sick rabbit? The hopital. What do the doctors do for him? Give him a hop-eration.

7. How does a rabbit love story end? They lived hoppily ever after.

8. What did the rabbit parents say when their children were grown up? That was a hare-raising experience.

A FEW JOKES FOR VARIOUS CATEGORIES

THREE JOKES ABOUT A MAN

1. What happened to the man who drank eight bottles of Coke? He burped "seven up."

2. What happened to the man who read a book about levitation? He couldn't put it down.

3. What happened to a man who swallowed a clock? For him, time passed slowly.

THREE SILLY JOKES

1. Why did the apple go out with a prune? Couldn't get a date!

2. How do sailors get their clothes clean? They throw them overboard and they wash ashore.

3. What do you get when you run over a canary with your lawn mower? Shredded tweet.

EVEN MORE SILLY JOKES

1. What do you get when you cross a nudist with a vegetarian? A person who refuses to put dressing on his salad.

2. What do you get when you cross a parakeet with a shark? An animal that bites your ear off.

3. What do you get when you cross an elephant with a kangaroo? Big holes all over Australia.

MUSIC JOKES

1. Why did Mozart spend the day in bed? He was writing sheet music.

2. What do you get when you cross Blackbeard the Pirate with a soprano from the opera? Mutiny on the high c`s.

3. We all know that the great musician, Beethoven went to the grave many years ago. Since then, what has he been doing? Decomposing.

4. Why did the piano player bang his head on the keys? He was playing by ear.

5. How do you clean a tuba? With a tube-a-toothpaste.

6. What do you call the father of a tuba? Oom-pa-pa.

GOVERNMENT JOKES

1. What is the difference between a politician and a thief? One takes the money and runs, the other runs, then takes the money.

2. What is the difference between a politician and a baseball player? When a baseball player gets caught stealing, he is out.

EVEN MORE SILLY JOKES

1. What do you call a camel with no humps? Humphrey.

2. What do you call people who can't stop themselves from stealing rugs? Rug addicts.

3. What is wrong with the number one hundred-forty-four? It is gross.

ACTUAL SIGNS

Sometimes road signs may not steer you right. Here's what I mean...

1. In the window of a Kentucky appliance store: "Don't kill your wife, let our washing machine do the dirty work."

2. On a Tennessee highway: "When this sign is under water, this road is impassable."

3. At a Pennsylvania cemetery: "Persons are prohibited from picking flowers from any but their own graves."

4. In a Florida maternity ward: "No children allowed."

5. In a Tacoma, Washington men's store: "15 men's wool suits! They won't last an hour!"

6. In a restaurant in Maine: "We are open seven days a week and weekends!"

7. Sign seen in a radiator shop: "This is the best place to take a leak."

YOU WOULDN'T THINK THESE JOKES WOULD WORK, BUT THEY DO...

I'm not sure why, but the following jokes almost always get a laugh. It may be because they are funny, or it may be people are just laughing at the fact that I dared to tell them!

A grandmother was surprised by her seven-year-old grandson one morning. He had made her a cup of coffee.
She drank it. It was the worst cup of coffee she had ever had. When she got to the bottom of the cup, she saw three little green army men, there in the cup.
She said, "Honey, what are the army men doing in my coffee?"
The grandson said, "Like it says on TV, the best part of waking up is soldiers in your cup." (Folgers in your cup)

One morning, I was in my backyard, when a giant rabbit approached me. I couldn't believe the sight. This bunny was ten feet tall!
He opened his mouth to bite me. His teeth were immense. Suddenly he disappeared. I mean, he completely vanished.
Then I realized, it was just a hop-tical illusion. (Optical)

Did you hear about the fly that buzzed into a cow's ear? It didn't come out again. In fact, it disappeared.
Then, three days later, when the cow was being milked, the fly popped out in the cow's milk.
What did the veterinarian say about this? He said it was "In one ear and out the udder!"

Did you hear about the professional illusionist who fell into one of his own trapdoors during a show? He got stuck halfway through. From the waist up, he was still in view. From the waist down, he was out of sight.
His assistants said this was nothing to worry about. It was just a stage that he was going through!

YOU WOULDN'T THINK THESE JOKES WOULD WORK, BUT THEY DO... (Continued)

A man was walking through the lobby of a fancy hotel, when suddenly, a glass eyeball fell into his hand. He looked up and saw a woman leaning over the balcony of the third floor. Obviously, her eye had fallen out.

The man quickly hurried up the stairs while the woman waited. When he finally came near her, she rushed forward and threw her arms around him. Then she gave him a huge kiss.

He was shocked and said, "Madam, do you do this with every man you meet?"

She replied, "Of course not, it is only with those who catch my eye!"

A man went to visit a friend. Upon entering the house, he discovered his friend standing in the living room with a fly swatter.

He said, "What are you doing?"

His friend said, "I'm killing flies. So far I've killed two males and three females."

The man asked, "How can you tell the difference?"

His friend replied, "It's easy. The two males were on the remote control, the three females were on the phone!"

FINALLY...

This book is meant to be a resource. Adapt the ideas. Play with the jokes and make them your own. Practice your lines and rehearse your delivery. Entertain people. It is a wonderful thing to do.

THE END

Looking for props, books, videos, and other stuff to use for entertainment purposes? Contact:

LAFLIN MAGIC
Box 3003
Troy, Montana 59935

406-295-7790